INDUSTRIAL AGE
MEDICINE

Rebecca Vickers

Chicago, Illinois

www.capstonepub.com
Visit our website to find out more information about Heinemann-Raintree books.

To order:

☎ Phone 800-747-4992

🖥 Visit www.capstonepub.com to browse our catalog and order online.

© 2013 Raintree
an imprint of Capstone Global Library, LLC
Chicago, Illinois

Edited by Andrew Farrow, Adam Miller, and Vaarunika Dharmapala
Designed by Philippa Jenkins
Picture research by Ruth Blair
Originated by Capstone Global Library Ltd
Printed and bound in China by Leo Paper Products Ltd

16 15 14 13 12
10 9 8 7 6 5 4 3 2 1

Library of Congress Cataloging-in-Publication Data
Vickers, Rebecca.
  Industrial age medicine / Rebecca Vickers.
    p. cm. — (Medicine through the ages)
  Includes bibliographical references and index.
  ISBN 978-1-4109-4645-4 (hb (freestyle)) — ISBN 978-1-4109-4651-5 (pb (freestyle)) 1. Medicine — History — 19th century. 2. Medicine — History — 18th century. 3. Industrial revolution. I. Title.
  R149.V53 2013
  610 — dc23   2011031908

Acknowledgments
We would like to thank the following for permission to reproduce photographs: Alamy pp. 6 (© North Wind Picture Archives), 12, 24, 29 (© The Protected Art Archive), 32 (© Paris Pierce), 33 (© Vario Images GmbH & Co. KG), 39 (© Photo Researchers); Corbis pp. 10 (© The Gallery Collection), 23 (© Bettmann); Courtesy of NLM p. 28; Getty Images pp. 18, 26, 27, 35 (Hulton Archive), 21 (Buyenlarge), 22 (MPI), 30 (SSPL), 36 (Museum of the City of New York); Mary Evans Picture Library p. 14; Science Photo Library pp. 19 (Jim Varney), 20, 38 (National Library of Medicine), Wellcome Library, London pp. 4, 5, 8, 9, 11, 16, 19, 25, 31, 34, 37, 41.

Cover photograph of a painting of Florence Nightingale tending to a patient at Scutari Barracks, Turkey, reproduced with permission of Alamy (© Mary Evans Picture Library).

Every effort has been made to contact copyright holders of any material reproduced in this book. Any omissions will be rectified in subsequent printings if notice is given to the publisher.

Contents

Some words are shown in bold, **like this**. You can find out what they mean by looking in the glossary. You can also look out for them in the "Word Station" box at the bottom of each page.

Medicine on the Move

By the mid-18th century, the profession of medicine was entering a period of rapid change and development. Many old ideas about the human body and how to cure and prevent diseases were being questioned. Doctors themselves were becoming better trained and more professional and organized in their approach.

This etching by William Hogarth is known as both *The Company of Undertakers* and *A Consultation of Physicians* (1736). It shows that doctors were traditionally viewed very negatively. They were seen as overpaid and lazy, and some were regarded as **quacks** who sold useless remedies. This view began to change in the mid-18th century, as the profession became more regulated.

Becoming a doctor

One of the routes a young man could follow to become a doctor was to attend college. The first medical school in North America, the Philadelphia Medical College, was founded in 1765. Other young men **apprenticed** themselves to a medical professional, while still others paid to attend private medical lectures. There were no set medical courses, no specific requirements, and only a few professional organizations.

Sticking to what they knew

Most of the equipment used by doctors had not changed very much in the previous 200 years. The methods used to **diagnose** patients were usually not scientific. The microscope (1590s) and the thermometer (1709) had both been invented, but doctors still preferred to poke and prod their patients and examine their urine. However, even if doctors *had* wanted to use the thermometer, until the mid-19th century this instrument was usually about 1 foot (30 centimeters) long and took half an hour to register a temperature.

The most advanced medical knowledge was in the field of **anatomy**. Most doctors attended **dissecting** rooms as part of their training.

Although some new instruments were available to doctors by 1750, most doctors could fit the equipment and treatments available to them into a leather case like this one.

Rapid changes

From the mid-18th century, there were many rapid changes in medical understanding, training, procedures, and equipment. Why were the conditions at this time so perfect for such a transformation?

The period we now call the Industrial Revolution was when the economy of countries began to change from the small-scale, local production of goods to large-scale factory production. This started during the second half of the 18th century. People moved from the country to work in the growing industries based in cities. The crowded and dirty living conditions there led to the spread of diseases and air and water pollution.

The Industrial Revolution led to **urbanization** and crowding. These conditions were the perfect breeding grounds for **contagious** diseases.

new drugs and treatments

overcrowding

technological advances

urbanization

contagious diseases

improved communication

Industrial Revolution

pollution

spread of new ideas

public health

brilliant individuals

nursing

wars

MEDICINE LEAPS FORWARD

improved treatments

professional training

This diagram shows the many factors that led to advances in medical science.

HERMAN BOERHAAVE
(1668–1738)

Herman Boerhaave was the first modern medical educator. He set the standards for **clinical** teaching, which is based on observing and treating patients. He created the idea of the teaching hospital. In addition to being a doctor, Boerhaave was a botanist (meaning he studied plant life) and head of the chemistry department at Leiden University, in the Netherlands.

Science and technology

Some of the technologies that came into use during the Industrial Revolution could be applied to scientific work as well as business. For example, better technology led to improvements in glass-making. This, in turn, made it possible to build microscopes with better lenses.

The medical profession was starting to see the advantages of learning about other sciences—and from other doctors. Doctors such as Herman Boerhaave, professor of medicine at Leiden University in the Netherlands, saw the importance of record keeping and using new scientific discoveries. These ideas spread as students and teachers moved between medical schools.

The work of brilliant and innovative individuals also had a huge impact on medical progress. Some, such as Louis Pasteur (see pages 16–17) and Robert Koch (see page 18), made discoveries and proved theories that would eventually change medicine forever.

Beginning to Understand Diseases

The most important change in medical practice was an increased understanding of what caused illness and disease. For thousands of years, the medical profession had believed that diseases were spread by invisible **contamination** that moved through the air. These clouds of death were known as *miasma*, an ancient Greek word meaning "pollution" or "stain."

Diseases in the air

The idea of disease-causing agents traveling in smelly or unpleasant air is not entirely wrong. Airborne **pathogens** that travel in the air and infect people do exist. But by focusing only on this, doctors missed other sources of infection. People held the false idea that using sweet herbs, candles, and torches to remove smells could protect against or prevent the spread of **contagious** diseases. This put people at risk for hundreds of years.

This is a state-of-the art microscope from the mid-18th century.

WORD STATION
miasma unpleasant or unhealthy substance in the air

Seeing the causes of disease

The improved microscope lenses of the mid-18th century meant that scientists could now see much smaller things. Some thought that very small living things, usually referred to as "animalcules," might have something to do with the spread of illnesses. John Pringle conducted research into **epidemics** in prisons, hospitals, and military camps. He recognized that the close confinement of large numbers of people resulted in a rapid spread of infections.

Could this have something to do with animalcules? Pringle had seen these through microscopes and he had read about them in the works of the Dutch scientist Anton van Leeuwenhoek. Pringle thought that these living agents could be the cause of the **dysentery** and typhus fevers he was eager to prevent. However, he could not see beyond miasma theory—he still thought that it was the air that had became rotten and infected.

JOHN PRINGLE
(1707-1782)

Pringle was a Scottish doctor and researcher. He worked tirelessly to stop the massive numbers of deaths that seemed to occur whenever large groups of people lived close together. His obsession with finding ways to prevent diseases from spreading led him to research **antiseptic** substances for the cleaning of surfaces, individuals, and their clothing.

Did you know?
John Pringle was the first to use the word *antiseptic* to mean something that works against and destroys anything septic (infected and rotten).

Inoculation

The most feared of all major diseases at the time was **smallpox**. This disease killed most of the people who caught it, and those who did not die were often left blind and hideously scarred, particularly on the face. Some people tried to protect themselves with the risky method of **inoculation**. This involved being deliberately infected with pus taken from the smallpox sores of someone suffering from a mild form of the disease.

MARY WORTLEY MONTAGU
(1689–1762)

Mary Montagu was an English aristocrat and wife of the ambassador to Turkey. While she was in Turkey, she witnessed smallpox inoculations. After her return, she introduced the method to England. Soon, people could pay to be inoculated. A piece of thread was soaked in pus taken from a smallpox **lesion**. It was then introduced into a cut in the arm of the patient. Patients would be isolated in a warm room until they had gone through a mild form of the disease. If the patients survived, they would be unlikely to catch smallpox again. However, there was always a risk that the smallpox inoculation would develop into a life-threatening form of the disease.

Did you know?
Montagu's letters home are a good source of information about life in the Ottoman Empire. This empire included Turkey and was one of the largest and most long-lasting empires in history.

WORD STATION
smallpox disease characterized by pus-filled blisters

This early 19th-century cartoon shows Edward Jenner vaccinating some worried patients. They are sprouting cow heads—a reference to Jenner's experiments with the cowpox vaccine.

Edward Jenner's cowpox experiments

English doctor Edward Jenner (1749–1823) believed that people who caught cowpox, a mild form of smallpox, never went on to get the deadlier version of the disease. Jenner noticed this effect in milkmaids who had regular contact with cows. In 1796, he used a healthy eight-year-old boy, James Phipps, to test his **hypothesis**.

Jenner collected pus from a cowpox scab on a milkmaid and put it in a cut on James's arm. James became a bit sick, but he recovered in a few days. Then, Jenner infected James with smallpox in the same way. Nothing happened! James's **vaccination** with cowpox *did* protect him from smallpox. Within a very short period of time, vaccination against smallpox spread around the world.

Cleaning Up Medicine

By using observation, **hypothesis**, and experimentation, Edward Jenner gave the medical world a tool in the fight against the dreadful disease **smallpox**. At the same time, other doctors were discovering more ways to keep diseases from spreading.

These soldiers from the Civil War (1861–1865) are dressing wounds in a makeshift hospital tent. Conditions such as this were dirty and dangerous.

John Pringle and others had noticed that diseases spread very quickly in crowded conditions. Diseases such as "jail fever" and "hospital fever" were rapidly transmitted between people, resulting in very high **mortality** rates.

However, doctors could only experiment with what *seemed* to work. They did not know why one experiment was successful and another a failure. This was because they did not know about **microbes**, the tiny living things that spread most diseases from one person to another.

Jail fever travels to the courts

Pringle recognized that typhus fevers were not only causing **epidemics** in jails. They also were traveling with inmates when they went to court! There were a number of cases of people who had been in court, including judges, contracting jail fever. Pringle introduced a set of measures that included washing inmates before they went to court and giving them new, clean clothes to wear. His reforms worked when they were put into practice, but he met with resistance to many of his calls for change.

Pringle's *Observations*

In 1744, Pringle was made physician general to the British Army. In 1752, the first edition of his *Observations on the Diseases of the Army* was published. This book was significant for putting into print Pringle's ideas about cross-infection between people and their belongings. He stressed this as a source of spreading disease.

COMMON CONFUSIONS

When the cure causes death

The lack of understanding about what caused diseases and infections meant that having any medical treatment was a major risk. There were exceptionally high death rates for most surgical procedures. This was because it was very easy for germs from dirty doctors, instruments, or linens to enter open wounds. This was also the case for childbirth and the treatment of injuries after battles.

This table shows how many years the average person could expect to live in these countries in 1800. What factors do you think account for the differences between nations?

Life expectancy at birth in 1800	
United Kingdom	40
United States	39
Germany	38
Australia	35
France	32
India	25

Germs: Small, but deadly

Many doctors and other scientists had seen living "animalcules" through microscopes or in drawings. Some, such as U.S. doctor John Crawford (1746–1813), thought these sources of transmission were members of the insect kingdom, with a similar life cycle: "Man has invisible, insect-like enemies, numerous and incapable of detection by the ordinary senses." However, there was a very strong resistance to the idea that these living things were causing and spreading diseases.

RIGHT IDEA, WRONG TIME

John Crawford suffered for promoting an idea ahead of its time. In an 1813 letter to another well-known U.S. doctor, Benjamin Rush, Crawford complained about his growing debts, saying he had lost all his business by "propagating [promoting] an unpopular opinion in medicine, namely that all diseases were occasioned [caused] by *animalculae*."

Animalcules.

These were some of the animalcules identified by scientists by 1794.

Ignaz Semmelweis

In 1844, Hungarian doctor Ignaz Semmelweis (1818–1865) began working at a hospital in Vienna, Austria. The hospital had two public maternity clinics. Semmelweis soon noticed that many more women were dying after childbirth in one of the clinics than in the other. One clinic was run by doctors from the hospital, while the other was run by midwives (people trained to assist in childbirth). Semmelweis was horrified when his **statistical** analysis of the deaths showed that it was the doctors who were making one of the clinics into a death trap.

While the midwives only delivered babies, the doctors also performed **autopsies** and **dissected** the bodies of women who had died during or after childbirth. They did not wash their hands or change their clothing between duties. Semmelweis did not understand how this was causing the spread of infection, but he decided to find ways to stop it. When he got the doctors to wash their hands in chloride of lime before touching living patients, the death rate fell rapidly. The washing was killing the germs that caused infections. However, Semmelweis's methods were not approved of, and he lost his job in 1849.

DOCTOR'S CLINIC

PERFORM AUTOPSIES

bad survival rates

HELP WOMEN GIVE BIRTH

MIDWIFE'S CLINIC

good survival rates

This diagram shows what Ignaz Semmelweis found to be the common and distinct factors between the clinic run by doctors and the clinic run by midwives.

The Proof of Germ Theory

By the 19th century, improved microscopes meant that many people had seen animalcules. However, most doctors and scientists believed that these **microbes** were created by diseases, not that they were the agents that *caused* diseases. This theory was called spontaneous generation. Then, a French scientist named Louis Pasteur (1822–1895) proved them wrong.

 This 1885 drawing shows Louis Pasteur using a microscope in his laboratory.

Proving the link

Pasteur was researching the reasons why alcohol would sometimes turn sour during the **fermentation** process. When he examined the liquid under a microscope, he could see living microbes. His **hypothesis** was that the germs were getting into the open vats of liquid through the air and **contaminating** it.

Pasteur put water into a special curved, "swan-neck" flask, then heated it to boiling. The boiling killed off any germs in the water, and the rising warm air was pushed out around the bend in the neck of the flask, taking any germs with it. No germs "spontaneously generated" in this water.

However, when the neck of the flask was broken and the previously **sterile** water was left open to the air, it once again became contaminated with germs.

Matching germs to diseases

This successful experiment proved a connection between specific germs and the contamination of the liquid. Armed with this knowledge, Pasteur very quickly went on to do several very important things:

- He developed methods to destroy and prevent contamination and infection, including pasteurization, where heating a liquid at specific temperatures for set lengths of time destroys germs, keeping it safe and fresh.

- He started to work on specific diseases, mostly those that affected animals, developing vaccines and other treatments. A major success was finding the germ that caused **rabies**, as well as a treatment for the disease.

- He convinced many doctors, particularly surgeons, that they should **sterilize** their equipment and instruments. This killed many of the germs that would have been transferred from patient to patient.

What are germs?

Using the word *germ* makes it sound as if there is just one type of thing that causes all diseases. In fact, there are many different types of microbes—including bacteria, viruses, and fungi—that cause contamination, infection, and specific diseases.

Seeking the microbes

Pasteur said the next step was to figure out which germ caused which disease—to "seek the microbe." Only then could treatments and preventions be developed. In 1872, the German doctor Robert Koch (1843–1910) started to do just that. Koch used his skills as a doctor as well as experimental methods. He used new technology, such as dyes to color microscopic slides and cameras to photograph his results. In this way, Koch identified anthrax (1876), septicemia (1878), tuberculosis (1882), and cholera (1883). The work of Koch and others made it possible to create vaccines and other treatments for some of the most deadly diseases.

Robert Koch started his medical career as a doctor in the Prussian army.

Joseph Lister

Joseph Lister (1827–1912) was a young professor of surgery at the University of Glasgow, in Scotland, when he became familiar with Pasteur's work in the mid-1860s. He realized that in addition to contaminating the brewing process, germs were also the cause of the infections that killed so many patients after surgery. How could he make an operating room a germ-free environment?

Joseph Lister used a disinfectant called carbolic acid in operating rooms like this one. The disinfectant was sprayed from the pump on the right.

More surgery, more death

When **anesthetics** became widely used at the end of the 1840s (see pages 22–23), doctors started performing more operations. They could also take more time, since they did not have to worry about the pain patients were suffering. However, this also meant that the rooms and instruments were being used for more people, plus the germs had more time to enter open wounds. Pain management had improved, but hygiene had not. In the 20 years after anesthetics were introduced, the death rate went up, not down. This is called the "Black Period" of surgery.

Lister knew he would have to find some way to kill germs. He started to experiment with carbolic acid, a disinfectant used to combat the odor of rotting sewage. Very quickly he realized he had hit upon something that worked. Soaking surgical bandages in carbolic acid meant that wounds were protected from infection. When all other parts of operating rooms were sprayed with carbolic acid, including the surgeons and the patients, the death rates fell dramatically.

Today, disinfectants are still used to keep germs out of hospitals.

Hospitals

In the early 19th century, hospitals were mostly for sick poor people, since other people were usually treated at home. Hospitals were dirty and crowded, and they provided very little in the way of useful medical treatments. However, during the next 100 years, hospitals changed dramatically.

What changed?

Three main developments during the 19th century changed hospitals:

- *Science changed*: Even before the gradual acceptance of germ theory in the 1870s and 1880s (see pages 16–19), John Pringle, Florence Nightingale (see pages 30–31), and Ignaz Semmelweis, among others, had stressed the need for cleanliness and order. The development of pain control methods such as **anesthetics** (see pages 22–23) meant that surgery could be more complex and take longer. The introduction of effective **antiseptics** from the late 1860s decreased deaths from the diseases and infections patients contracted in hospitals. Hospitals really were safer.

As shown in this illustration from 1807, until the 1850s, nurses were often untrained and incompetent. Nursing was not considered a profession, and many nurses were glorified babysitters of the sick and dying.

By the time this military hospital in Washington, D.C., was open in 1865, hospitals were safer, better equipped, and staffed by medical professionals.

- *Technology developed*: Laboratory testing of samples, specialized clinics, and eventually very large machinery such as X-ray machines meant that hospitals offered services that were not available elsewhere.

- *Training of medical professionals became more **systematic***: During the 19th century, the medical profession started to organize itself. Teaching hospitals became the norm. Attending lectures, visiting patients, and doing research in hospitals formed part of every doctor's professional development. Medical groups started setting standards and membership requirements. In 1847 Dr. Nathan Smith Davis founded the American Medical Association (AMA). The first UK school for nurse training, the Institution of Nursing Sisters, was founded by Elizabeth Fry in 1840. The first nursing programs in the United States did not start until the 1870s, but by 1900, there were 10,000 professional nurses!

ELIZABETH FRY
(1780–1845)

Elizabeth Fry was born into a Quaker family in Norwich, England, and from a young age she was involved in **philanthropic** activities. She promoted **smallpox vaccination** and worked tirelessly for prison improvements, particularly for women's prisons. After visiting a nursing school in Germany in 1840, she returned to England and founded the Institution for Nursing Sisters.

Did you know?
Fry was **dyslexic** and overcame her educational problems to focus on helping others.

Preventing pain

Operations done without anesthetics had to be performed quickly with only the aid of **opiates** and alcohol to lessen the pain. The pain itself could be unbearable to the patient, and the shock of the pain could also prove fatal.

In the mid-1840s, Horace Wells, a dentist working in Connecticut, wanted to make his patients more comfortable during dental treatments. He started experimenting with inhaled nitrous oxide gas to make his patients woozy or unconscious. He had mixed success. Another dentist, William Morton, working in Boston, Massachusetts, had better luck with another gas, called ether. In October 1846, he gave ether to a patient while a surgeon removed a tumor from the patient's neck. This public operation was a painless success. Within two months, ether was also being used in the United Kingdom.

A NEW NAME

The word *anesthetic* is derived from a Greek word for "insensibility." It was given to the new method of pain relief by U.S. doctor Oliver Wendell Homes, Sr., in 1846.

Ether is being used on this patient during an operation in Boston in 1846.

WORD STATION
opiate drug containing opium or made from opium

Chloroform got a boost in popularity when Queen Victoria (seated) of the United Kingdom used it in 1853 during the birth of her eighth child. She referred to the effects of the chloroform as "soothing, quieting, and delightful beyond measure."

ROBERT LISTON
(1794–1847)

Scottish surgeon Robert Liston was the first in the United Kingdom to use ether during major surgery. On December 21, 1846, he amputated the leg of Frederick Churchill using ether as an anesthetic. The patient felt no pain, and Liston was converted to the use of anesthetics.

Did you know?
Liston was legendary for the speed of his surgery, usually amputating limbs in under a minute!

WHAT WAS WRONG WITH ETHER?

James Simpson disliked ether for several reasons:
- It was a highly flammable gas.
- It irritated some patients' lungs, causing them to cough during surgery.
- It had a very strong and unpleasant smell.

Chloroform is better

James Young Simpson (1811–1870) was the professor of Midwifery at Edinburgh University, in Scotland. He decided that there must be a substance that would relieve pain like ether, but that did not have its bad points. His experiments, including testing on himself and his colleagues, led him in late 1847 to chloroform. It was stronger and faster acting than ether, and it was easier to give to patients. Although there were those who disapproved of making a patient unconscious to prevent pain, it gradually gained support. Chloroform was the most common anesthetic used until 1900. Ether then came back into favor when it was shown that chloroform use could permanently damage the liver and cause heart attacks and breathing difficulties.

The Growth of Public Health

The Industrial Revolution began in the second half of the 18th century in the United Kingdom. It led to **urbanization**, population growth, poverty, and pollution. As the major cities grew, the living conditions of the urban poor worsened. The UK government did nothing to provide better water supplies or remove garbage and sewage. Typhoid fever, tuberculosis, and influenza were commonplace. Then, cholera arrived.

Government jumps in

By the end of the first great cholera **epidemic** in the United Kingdom in 1832, over 20,000 people had died. The government eventually tried to fight this horrific disease. Regulations were enforced requiring immediate burial of cholera victims, and local Boards of Health were set up to try to find methods of dealing with it. Since the disease was still believed to spread through a **miasma**, barrels of tar were burned in city streets in attempts to "purify" the air. However, nothing worked. Death by cholera occurred so fast it was commonly said that people could be well at breakfast and dead by dinner.

COMMON CONFUSIONS

What is cholera?

Cholera is an infectious bacterial disease that affects the intestines, causing diarrhea, abdominal cramping, vomiting (throwing up), **dehydration**, and a high fever. Over 60 percent of untreated people who catch it die. Doctors at the time of the first outbreaks in the 19th century had no idea what caused it, how it could be cured, or how to stop it from spreading.

These crowded homes on the Lower East Side of New York City were a breeding ground for disease and death (see pages 28–29).

WORD STATION
dehydration condition caused by not having enough water in the body

In this drawing from 1849, the clothes of cholera victims are being burned and thrown in the river in Exeter, England. Drinking water for the city came from the river. In 1832, no one knew that cholera was passed through water.

In the years after the 1832 epidemic, various reports, some ordered by the government, confirmed that most of the urban poor lived in dirty, unhealthy conditions. Pressure was growing for what became known as "sanitary reform"—cleaning up towns and cities by improving water supplies, sewage, garbage collection, and living conditions. Many politicians opposed the government getting involved in people's lives in this way and were against passing a Public Health Bill.

Not again!

Then, after over 15 years without a great epidemic, cholera struck the United Kingdom again in 1848. The Public Health Bill was finally approved. The Public Health Act set up voluntary Boards of Health all over the country. If there was support, then a local board could set about improving the water and sewage systems.

John Snow figures it out

The next big cholera outbreak in London, England, struck in 1854. Most doctors and politicians still believed that cholera was transmitted in bad, smelly air. However, London doctor John Snow had written an article in 1849 suggesting that cholera entered the body through the mouth. When the new outbreak started, Snow plotted every case that occurred on a map, to try to show where the disease started. He traced the disease to a public water pump. When he ordered the pump handle removed, the number of cases of cholera fell. Cholera *was* spread through the water and into victims' mouths, not through the air!

EDWIN CHADWICK
(1800–1890)

Edwin Chadwick was a British social reformer. He collected information about the living conditions of the urban poor, particularly in the East End of London. His report shocked the country. Chadwick was convinced that if it were possible to make cities cleaner, then people in cities would be healthier, would be able to work harder, and would cost the government less money in relief payments to the poor.

Did you know?
Chadwick was a firm believer in the miasma theory. He thought if London got rid of its foul smell, everyone's health would improve.

The Great Stink of 1858

Once John Snow had confirmed that cholera was carried in water, it became even more important that something be done to make the water safer in London. It was the biggest city in the world, with a population of over 2.75 million. However, nothing had been done to solve the water and sewage mess.

The huge building project that gave London a functioning sewer system was planned and built under the control of Joseph Bazalgette (1819–1891), standing top right. When he died, an obituary claimed that he had added 20 years to the lifespan of every Londoner.

By the summer of 1858, the Thames River had become filled with human and animal waste. Waterborne diseases, such as cholera and typhoid, were common. The smell had become overwhelmingly horrible and became known as the "Great Stink" of 1858. Suddenly, the misguided fear of cholera from the miasma of smell in the city gave the authorities the push they needed. London would finally get the sewer system it so desperately needed. The last bad outbreak of cholera in London was in 1866. By 1868, after 10 years, the sewers and water supply systems were finished.

What is a tenement?

The word *tenement* often makes people think of crowded, poverty-stricken city slums, but it originally meant any rented building. In 1867, New York state law gave "tenement" a specific legal definition: a building lived in independently by three or more families or by more than two families on a floor.

New York City

The Industrial Revolution also spread to other parts of the world. As a result, other countries were also affected by dirty and crowded cities. In the United States, New York City expanded from 60,000 citizens in 1800 to over 3.5 million by 1900, as wave after wave of immigrants swelled its population. As its population grew, so did its public health problems.

Epidemics of yellow fever struck the city in 1795, 1799, and 1803, killing many. In 1805, authorities set up a Board of Health to examine ways to protect people. But over the next 50 years, the board only reacted if something terrible happened, such as an epidemic. By 1850, the average life expectancy (age at death) for a New Yorker was only 20 years, 8 months!

This cartoon from the time makes fun of the first New York Board of Health. It only reacted when disaster struck, and it did not plan for the future.

OUR NEW YORK BOARD OF HEALTH.

People who lived in tenements, such as these children, experienced a combination of poverty, filth, and overcrowding. They also faced corrupt landlords and government officials. Many children in the tenements died from **malnutrition**.

The 1866 Metropolitan Bill of Health

From 1859 to 1866, social reformers had pushed for an independent group to solve New York City's disastrous public health situation. In 1866, the Metropolitan Bill of Health gave power to a commission appointed by the state governor (with some doctors as members), but this was only temporary. By 1870, the **corrupt** mayor of the city was back in charge.

Public pressure for change meant that improvements did start to happen, at least in the control of diseases and supply of clean water. By the end of the century, the tenement slums (see the box on page 28) were still present. But a **systematic** approach was being taken to prevent and control diseases, and food and drinks such as milk were inspected to make sure they were healthy and safe to eat or drink.

War and Changes in Medicine

During the 19th century, three major wars had an impact on changes that took place in medicine: the Crimean War, the U.S. Civil War, and the Franco-Prussian War.

The Crimean War (1853–1856)

The Crimean War was fought between the Russian Empire and an alliance including the United Kingdom and France. The war is often remembered for British nurse Florence Nightingale.

In 1854, Nightingale and 38 others nurses went to the Turkish port of Scutari, where sick and wounded British soldiers were treated. Nightingale wanted to improve the recovery rates of the wounded soldiers. She found the conditions there dirty and overcrowded, with uncooperative workers and few medical supplies.

Out on the battlefields of the mid-19th century, a surgeon often had to amputate mangled limbs with saws like these.

By 1856, Nightingale had put in place new measures and methods of treatment. Hygiene was greatly improved, and conditions were less crowded. As a result, the death rate fell from 42 percent to only 2 percent. However, it was after Nightingale returned to England that she had the most impact.

- She used money from a public fund set up in her name to develop and set standards for the training of nurses.

- She wrote the book that became the training manual for the profession, *Notes on Nursing* (1859).

- She gave evidence to the government and wrote many recommendations as to how the army medical services should be improved and organized, and how soldiers should be treated.

- She championed the cause of "sanitary reform," meaning the importance of hygiene and improving living conditions in order to promote health and prevent disease.

Florence Nightingale became famous as the "lady with the lamp" in Scutari. She would often wander the hospital at night to make sure the patients were being taken care of.

Was Scutari a triumph for Nightingale?

In 1857, Florence Nightingale examined **statistical** information about deaths in the Crimea. She realized many deaths during 1854–1855 had been caused by hospital conditions and not by battlefield injuries and **malnutrition**. Although she made sure that men were treated for injuries, **deloused**, and given clean clothes and blankets, it was overcrowding, bad sanitation, and lack of ventilation (the movement of air) that spread fevers and infections. In 1857 she said that "disease was chiefly generated within the building [hospital] itself." Total UK losses in the Crimea were 16,000 from sickness, 2,600 battlefield deaths, and 1,800 wounded.

The Civil War (1861–1865)

In the United States, the huge numbers of men involved in the Civil War created new problems and challenges for those whose task it was to treat the injured. Organizational and **logistical** changes were made by the Union Army during the war that are still part of the way medical services are run in modern armed forces. Most of these changes and innovations were the work of one man, Jonathan Letterman (1824–1872). Starting the war as a surgeon, by June 1862 he was the medical director of the entire Union Army. He introduced:

- an ambulance corps with trained stretcher bearers and wagon drivers to move the wounded away from the action

- three different treatment stations—a first aid treatment area on the battlefield, small battlefield hospitals near the fighting for emergency surgery and other required treatment, and large hospitals away from the fighting for long-term treatment, recovery, and rehabilitation

- the concept of **triage**, in which the wounded are categorized, with attention given first to those most likely to survive.

During the Civil War, organized transportation for the injured was provided by the Army of the Potomac's ambulance corps.

WORD STATION
logistical relating to providing facilities, moving people, and obtaining supplies

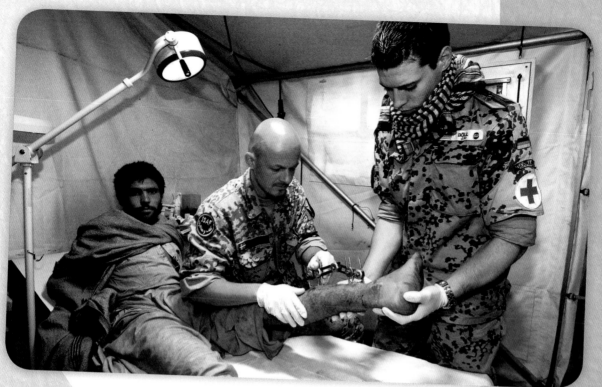

Just as in the past, modern war zones, such as Afghanistan, require medical workers to perform in difficult conditions.

The Franco-Prussian War (1870–1871)

The Franco-Prussian War was a short conflict between France and the German states. France eventually lost, and the war led to the unification of Germany. The two countries remained rivals after the conflict had ended.

At this time, each country had a famous medical scientific researcher: Louis Pasteur in France and Robert Koch in Germany. Each new discovery made by one of these men added to the national prestige of his country. The money and support that each man received from his country was good for the future of medicine, but it was also the result of continuing national tension and rivalry.

Each man was given enough money to support a research team, and research institutes for them to work in were founded in each country: the Institute Pasteur in France (1887) and the Institute for Infectious Diseases in Germany (1891).

NEUTRAL MEDICINE

Before the end of the 18th century, John Pringle got warring sides to agree to the neutrality of battlefield hospitals and their workers, meaning they did not take sides. This continues today through medical charities in war zones, such as the Red Cross.

Women and Medicine

By the mid-19th century, many jobs were still considered unsuitable for women. Teaching, being a companion, or being a governess were all that a woman could realistically hope for. However, things were beginning to change.

Making nursing a proper job

When Florence Nightingale told her parents that she wanted to become a nurse, they were horrified. She said, "It was as if I wanted to be a kitchen maid." They thought of nurses as either nuns or the old, lazy, drunken women portrayed by authors of the time. In 1856, Nightingale set up her first nursing training school at St. Thomas's Hospital in London.

Before Florence Nightingale (seated at the center, in a shawl), these young women would not have had a chance to become members of a respected profession.

LINDA RICHARDS
(1841–1930)

Linda Richards was the first American woman to professionally train as a nurse. Having nursed her own mother and her fiancé on their deathbeds, she joined the first group of five women to attend nurse training at the New England Hospital for Women and Children in Boston. After graduating in 1873, she worked for a year and then dedicated the rest of her working life to the promotion and establishment of quality nurse training colleges across the United States.

Soon schools of nursing sprung up at hospitals all over the United Kingdom. This proved that Nightingale had identified a real need, and nursing soon became a socially acceptable profession for respectable women. As we have seen, by the 1870s nursing schools began to spread across the United States, and by 1900 they were very popular.

Women dentists

The 19th century also saw the acceptance of women into training programs that allowed them to become fully qualified dentists. Some women had **apprenticed** themselves to dentists and learned on the job. Then, in 1865, an American woman, Lucy Hobbs Taylor (1833–1910), entered the Ohio College of Dental Surgery. Taylor had trained as a dentist through private study and had practiced dentistry in Ohio and Iowa. After the Iowa State Dental Society allowed her to join, this official acceptance helped her gain formal training and full qualifications.

WORD STATION
apprentice person who learns a trade or profession by working an agreed-upon period of time for someone who is

35

At last, Dr. Blackwell

When women first attempted to become doctors, the biggest obstacle in their path was getting accepted into a medical school. In 1870, less than 1 percent of U.S. women attended college. This was the problem that faced U.S. teacher Elizabeth Blackwell (1821–1910) when she decided to become a doctor.

The UK-born 26-year-old was rejected by 29 medical schools before starting at the Geneva Medical School in New York. She graduated at the top of her class in 1849. Blackwell went on to receive further training in Paris and London, before setting up the New York Infirmary for Women and Children in 1857. She worked in hospitals and as a medical educator for the rest of her life, inspiring young women to believe there was a place for them in medicine.

Male students and professors refused to attend classes when Blackwell started her training.

▶

By setting up medical schools and hospitals, like this one pictured in the 1920s, British nurse turned doctor Elizabeth Garrett Anderson made sure women could get medical training.

From nurse to doctor

One of those women inspired to become a doctor by Elizabeth Blackwell was British nurse Elizabeth Garrett Anderson (1836–1917). For four years she applied to every college and hospital in England to study medicine, but she was rejected by them all. She then followed a course of private study and then officially became a doctor in 1865.

Anderson developed a large medical practice and set up several teaching hospitals that trained women, later employing Elizabeth Blackwell as one of her lecturers.

The Brain, the Mind, and Medicine

At the beginning of the Industrial Revolution, knowledge of the workings of the brain was limited, and attitudes toward mental illnesses and conditions were influenced by superstition and religion. By the end of the 19th century, the science of **neurobiology** was well established and terms such as **psychiatry**, **psychology**, and **psychoanalysis** were familiar to specialists.

Mapping the brain

During the 19th century, great steps forward were taken in understanding and mapping the brain. Doctors performed experiments on animals and observed patients with injuries to specific parts of the brain. This made it clear that different parts of the brain were involved in different body functions. As early as 1811, Scottish surgeon Charles Bell figured out that nerves for the senses could be traced from the sense organs to specific parts of the brain. In 1862, French scientist Paul Broca located the position in the brain of the speech center. By 1874, German Carl Wernicke's study of stroke victims and their problems mapped out the brain even further.

Although care of the mentally ill was still very basic in the late 19th century, in most countries patients were no longer chained, starved, and filthy. This picture was taken in 1900 at the Boston Insane Hospital.

WORD STATION
psychoanalysis theory of how to treat mental disorders, focusing on the conscious mind (what someone knows she or he is thinking) and the unconscious mind (what someone does not know she or he is thinking)

Sigmund Freud argued that the mind contains both conscious and unconscious levels, and that feelings and thoughts can be hidden in the unconscious only to surface in a patient's dreams. He analyzed these dreams in order to uncover his patient's true desires. His theories were often controversial, but they influenced thinkers throughout the 20th century and in many fields beyond psychology.

A MEDICAL MARVEL

The story of Phineas Gage (1823–1860) revealed a lot about the workings of the brain. Gage was a U.S. railroad construction foreman who was injured in an 1848 dynamite explosion. The blast thrust a long metal bar through one side of his skull and out the other. Gage survived and quickly regained his physical and intellectual abilities. However, after the accident, his personality completely changed. He was subject to violent episodes, mood swings, and excessive swearing. Gage's injuries and the effects they had on him helped pinpoint the part of the brain—the frontal lobe—that controls personality traits and social **inhibitions**.

It's all in the mind

The renowned U.S. doctor Benjamin Rush (1746–1813) identified various psychiatric illnesses, including addiction, as early as 1812. However, it was not until the late 1800s that German doctors such as Wilhelm Wundt and Emil Kraepelin started to research and classify mental disorders. Schizophrenia (a breakdown in logical thinking) and bipolar disorder (a form of depression) were first described at this time.

By the 1880s, Jean Marie Charcot (1825–1893), and later his famous student, Sigmund Freud (1856–1939), developed the theories and treatments that became known as psychoanalysis. By 1900, the science of the mind was expanding in many directions.

The Medical Revolution

The years from the beginning of the Industrial Revolution to the dawning of the 20th century are often called the "medical revolution." However, the revolution did not happen by chance. A number of conditions developed and factors coincided that created the perfect circumstances for medicine to make huge advances.

Out with the old...

The most important thing that happened during this period was the triumph of germ theory over the idea of **contagious** disease spreading through **miasma**. Once this was understood and accepted by a majority of the medical profession, it was possible to try to prevent the spread of diseases and to develop treatments.

MEDICINE AROUND THE WORLD

By 1900, medical advances in the industrialized countries of the world had largely passed by those places that remained less developed. The continuing colonial rule by Western nations of much of the non-industrialized world brought some new ideas and treatments to these places. However, these practices were often available only to the rich and powerful. Christian medical missionaries were more likely to help the poor, but they expected people to convert to Christianity in return for treatment.

Organized compassion

The 1800s saw the birth of one of the most important U.S. humanitarian organizations—the American Red Cross.

Clara Barton (see page 32) traveled to Europe after the Civil War and was very impressed by the work of the Swiss-based Red Cross. Back in the United States, she campaigned for the country to have its own Red Cross Society.

In 1881, Barton and 23 others founded the American Red Cross Society. The new society campaigned for the adoption of the Geneva Convention (a treaty that protected those injured in war). A year later, in 1882, Congress ratified (approved) the Convention. The American Red Cross added disaster relief to the mission of the worldwide Red Cross movement. This is known as the "American Amendment."

In the 19th century, a new invention was introduced that is now the emblem of doctors everywhere—the stethoscope. The object shown here is a monaural stethoscope, an early form of the instrument. The round base of this stethoscope carried sound up the tube to the ear piece.

In with the new

The new **antiseptics**, starting with carbolic acid, gave medical professionals one of the most important tools they needed to halt the massive infection rates and to make surgery safer. Pain was finally conquered by **anesthetics**, and hospitals were no longer places of fear and death. Politicians, doctors, and engineers worked together to improve living conditions in cities. Doctors and nurses became members of well-regulated and respected professions.

However, the greatest contribution to the medical revolution came from the ideas, inventions, innovations, and discoveries of exceptional and gifted individuals. Their insights, determination, and hard work benefited everyone.

RENÉ LAËNNEC
(1781–1826)

René Laënnec was a French doctor who is remembered for having invented the monaural (one ear) stethoscope in 1816. He came up with the simple idea when he was having trouble listening to the chest of a very overweight female patient with a heart condition. His first design was a plain wooden tube. Later, he made one in three pieces that could be taken apart. In 1851, a binaural (two ear) stethoscope was developed by Arthur Leared, which is almost the same as the one used today.

Timeline

1751	A general hospital for the sick is founded in Philadelphia. It is the first hospital in the North American colonies.
1765	The first medical school in North America, the Philadelphia Medical College (now part of the University of Pennsylvania), is founded
1796	English doctor Edward Jenner introduces his **vaccination** against **smallpox**
1812	The *New England Journal of Medicine* starts publication. It is the first modern medical journal.
1816	The stethoscope is invented by René Laënnec
1818–1865	Life of Ignaz Semmelweis, the Hungarian doctor who discovered that doctors were spreading diseases
1832	The first great cholera **epidemics** occur in the United States and the United Kingdom
1843	The Association for Improving Conditions of the Poor is formed in New York City
1843–1910	Life of German medical researcher Robert Koch, who developed and proved the germ theory of disease
1845	U.S. dentist Horace Wells first uses ether as an **anesthetic** to relieve pain
1846	Anesthetics are first used in surgery
1847	Chloroform is used in childbirth as an anesthetic
1847	The American Medical Association (AMA) is founded by Dr. Nathan Smith Davis
1853–1856	Crimean War
1854	John Snow in London figures out that water is responsible for the spread of cholera, not a **miasma** of disease in the air
1855	Florence Nightingale starts to improve UK nursing and military conditions

1861–1865	U.S. Civil War
1861–1865	U.S. nurse Clara Barton becomes a national hero for her work to help soldiers during the Civil War
1865	Carbolic acid is first used as an **antiseptic** in surgery
1866	The Metropolitan Bill of Health is passed by the New York state legislature, setting up a comprehensive health commission for New York City
1868	The AMA Council on Ethics allows entry for qualified female doctors
1870	Joseph Lister's antiseptic spray is widely used in operations from this time
1870–1871	Franco-Prussian War
1876	Dr. Sarah Stephenson is the first female member of the AMA
late 1870s	Germ theory, as developed by Pasteur and Koch, becomes widely accepted by scientists and medical professionals
1885	Louis Pasteur develops a **rabies** vaccine
1887	Hermann Biggs and T. Mitchell Prudden identify the cholera bacteria
1892	The Bacteriological Laboratory of New York City is established under the leadership of Hermann Biggs, the first city lab in the world set up to **diagnose** diseases
1895	Aspirin is first produced by the German company Bayer
1895	Austrian psychiatrist Sigmund Freud publishes first work on **psychoanalysis**
1895	Wilhelm Roentgen makes the famous first X-ray of his wife's hand
1895	Free diphtheria antitoxins are given to the poor of New York City
1897	Ronald Ross proves that malaria is carried by a certain kind of mosquito
1900	Over 800,000 New Yorkers receive free smallpox vaccines

Glossary

anatomy science of the structure of the human body

anesthetic substance used in operations to stop a patient from feeling pain

antiseptic substance that prevents infection or contamination from germs and microbes

apprentice person who learns a trade or profession by working an agreed-upon period of time for someone who is trained

autopsy examination of a body to find out about the cause of death

clinical based on observation and treatment of patients

contagious able to be caught or passed from one person to another

contamination impurity from contact with something dirty or infected

corrupt dishonest

dehydration condition caused by not having enough water in the body

delouse clean someone of body and head lice

diagnose identify the nature of a disease or injury through examination

dissect cut up a dead body in order to examine it

dysentery serious infectious intestinal disease that causes violent, bloody diarrhea

dyslexic having a disorder involving difficulty in learning to read and write or interpret words and letters

epidemic rapid spread of a disease through an area or population

fermentation chemical change brought about by addition of a fermenting agent, such as yeast

hypothesis theory or unproven idea

inhibition suppression of certain behaviors or impulses that could be considered inappropriate

inoculation another term for vaccination

lesion pus-filled scab or sore, also known as a "pox"

logistical relating to providing facilities, moving people, and obtaining supplies

malnutrition condition caused by not having enough healthy, nutritious food

miasma unpleasant or unhealthy substance in the air

microbe very tiny living thing that can carry disease

mortality death

neurobiology branch of biology that deals with the nervous system

opiate drug containing opium or made from opium

pathogen bacterium, virus, or other microbe that can cause disease

philanthropic characterized by concern for others

psychiatry branch of medicine that deals with the diagnosis and treatment of mental disorders

psychoanalysis theory of how to treat mental disorders, focusing on the conscious mind (what someone knows she or he is thinking) and the unconscious mind (what someone does not know she or he is thinking)

psychology science of the mind, mental states, and mental processes

quack unqualified person who claims to have medical knowledge

rabies disease of the nervous system caused by germs transferred in the bite of an infected animal

smallpox disease characterized by pus-filled blisters

statistical using numerical data to arrive at a conclusion

sterile free of bacteria

sterilize make free of bacteria

systematic doing something in an ordered, organized, and consistent way

triage assigning priority by urgency to wounds or illnesses, in order to treat a large number of patients

urbanization growth of cities and towns

vaccination introducing a preparation (called a vaccine) into the body to create antibodies so the vaccinated person becomes immune and does not catch a disease

Find Out More

Books

Ballard, Carol. *From Cowpox to Antibiotics: Discovering Vaccines and Medicine* (Chain Reactions). Chicago: Heinemann Library, 2006.

Clare, John D. *Medicine in the Industrial World* (History of Medicine). New York: Enchanted Lion, 2006.

Hartman, Eve, and Wendy Meshbesher. *The Scientists Behind Medical Advances* (Sci-Hi Scientists). Chicago: Raintree, 2011.

Vickers, Rebecca. *Medicine* (From Fail to Win!). Chicago: Raintree, 2011.

Web sites

www.johnsnowsociety.org/johnsnow/facts.html
This web site will give you a lot of information about Dr. John Snow and his work to trace the source of cholera epidemics.

www.knowitall.org/kidswork/hospital/history/17_19century/index.html
This history of medicine includes facts about the industrial age.

nmhm.washingtondc.museum/exhibits/nationswounds
This web site of the National Museum of Health and Medicine explores medicine during the Civil War. Learn more facts about medicine during the war and see lots of interesting photos here.

www.tenement.org
This is the web site of the Lower East Side Tenement Museum. It gives you virtual tours and lots of information about life in the poor areas of New York City in the 19th century.

Places to visit

International Museum of Surgical Science, Chicago, Illinois
www.imss.org

National Museum of Civil War Medicine, Frederick, Maryland
www.civilwarmed.org

National Museum of Health and Medicine, Washington, D.C.
nmhm.washingtondc.museum

The Tenement Museum, New York City
www.tenement.org

More topics to research

Learn more about discoveries, technical advances, and events:

- improved microscope lenses

- improvements in sewage treatment and water supplies

- the X-ray

- medical and nursing schools

- infant mortality and the "swill milk" scandal in New York City

- government involvement in public health.

Learn more about people who made a difference:

- Dr. Nathan Smith Davis and U.S. medical training

- Dr. Hermann Biggs and health in U.S. cities

- John Pitard and New York City mortality statistics

- Dr. Elisha Harris and Dr. John Griscom's work to improve New York tenement life

- The cover of this book shows a detail from a painting of Florence Nightingale helping a patient at Scutari Barracks, Turkey. Find out more about how Nightingale changed the study and practice of nursing after she returned to England.

Index